Francis of Assisi

by
Jennifer Moorcroft

*All booklets are published thanks to the
generous support of the members of the
Catholic Truth Society*

CATHOLIC TRUTH SOCIETY
PUBLISHERS TO THE HOLY SEE

Contents

Wild Youth

In the autumn of 1997 an earthquake hit Umbria. The basilica of Saint Francis in Assisi was severely damaged, including the priceless frescoes by Giotto depicting the life of the little Poor Man of Assisi. Since then, experts have been painstakingly piecing the fragments together.

The frescoes tell the story of one who has been described as being, after Our Lady, most like Christ; of how this 'poverello' (poor man), restored the Gospel message to the heart of the Church as it emerged, battered, from the Dark Ages.

The story began in 1181/82 (the year is disputed), in the house of Pietro and Pica Bernadone. For one who would later seek to be the poorest of men, his birth was in a wealthy home. Pietro Bernadone was a merchant of fine cloth, not a nobleman, but one who aspired to join that august class, if not for himself, then for his sons. At the time of his elder son's birth he was away in France on business, so it was the Lady Pica who, a few days later, took her son to the nearby church of San Rufino to be baptised. He was given the name of Giovanni, (John); Francis, as he is always known, was a nickname perhaps given by his father, returning from France, or later because of Francis' love of all things French.

The story is told that as the Lady Pica was in bed after childbirth, a pilgrim came to the door begging for food. He then asked to see the newborn child and embracing him made the prophecy, 'Today two infants have been born in this street; one shall be among the best of this world, the other shall be among the worst.' Down that same street was born the child who would be called Brother Elias, whom we shall meet later on.

The troubadour

Francis proved to be a popular boy, with an air of gaiety and high spirits, charming and affectionate. He received a basic education at nearby St George's School, but his main education was helping out at his father's shop selling the rich cloth and joining him on his journeys to buy cloth, especially in France. As he grew up, he became the undisputed leader of the high-spirited youth of Assisi, causing considerable headaches for the good citizens of the city when their sleep was disturbed by carousing. Francis later looked back on this time of his life with deep remorse, and there has been some speculation as to how far his wildness went. The answer perhaps lies in his character, profoundly influenced by the troubadour tradition coming from the Languedoc.

Francis loved the French songs celebrating knightly courtesy and chivalry, especially towards women; the troubadour tradition stressed courtesy and nobility, and so simply reinforced qualities that were innate to his character.

That courtesy and nobility extended to the least as well as to the greatest, as it always would. One day, selling cloth at his father's shop to a wealthy patron, a beggar came up asking for alms. Francis ignored him, intent on the business in hand; but later, struck with remorse, he left the shop and the other customers and sought out the beggar to give him alms. He resolved from then on never to send anyone away empty handed.

Pietro Bernadone was gratified by his son's popularity, even if he sometimes protested at the lavishness with which the boy spent his father's money. Pietro was not as wealthy as the nobles with whom Francis consorted, but dreamt that his son might one day be admitted into their ranks – if money could ease the way. So he encouraged Francis to dress extravagantly and richly, since that told the world how well off Pietro Bernadone was.

Call to arms

Francis was not only enamoured of courtly love, but also of chivalry. He longed to be a knight fighting in battle. He had his wish when he was about fifteen. At that time much of Italy was part of the Holy Roman Empire, ruled over by the German Emperor, Frederick Barbarossa. When he died in 1197, to be succeeded by Henry VI, the resultant confusion was an opportunity for the Italians to rise up in revolt. What could be called the middle class in that feudal society – free men, artisans, craftsmen, merchants such as Pietro – had already organised itself into Communes and their wealth and influence were challenging the status quo of the nobility. They now rose up to form their own Communal Government. They executed or forced out the ruling aristocracy, who fled to the neighbouring town of Perugia. Perugia and the ousted aristocracy then took up arms against Assisi and civil war broke out. The struggle lasted for ten years, but when it began Francis eagerly answered the call to arms.

His war proved to be short lived for he was soon taken prisoner and spent about a year as a hostage in Perugia. He received a nobility of sorts because in his rich apparel he was assumed to be a noble and was imprisoned with the knights. He did not lose his gaiety among a despondent group who thought him mad, asking why he should make a joke of his situation. 'Why should I be miserable,' replied Francis to general laughter, 'when I think of the future that awaits me, when I know that one day I shall be the idol of the whole world?' His dreams of glory were real, but would not be as he imagined.

Prisoner of war

His gift of friendship and empathy was undimmed among the group of knights. One young man was so unpleasant that everyone except Francis avoided him. Francis' kindness and charm so won him over that he was able to raise his spirits and bring him back into the group.

He was eventually released in November 1203, but perhaps due to his imprisonment his always fragile health gave way and he spent some weeks in bed. When he was at last able to walk around with the help of sticks, he found he no longer took pleasure in his usual pursuits or even in the beautiful Umbrian countryside that he so loved. However, he still clung to dreams of chivalric glory, and when he heard that the Pope, Innocent III, was gathering an army to fight against Henry VI who was trying to gain the upper hand against the Papacy, he immediately made plans to join the Pontifical army.

Knight to a new Lord

Of course, no son of Pietro Bernadone could ride into battle less than magnificently equipped, so Francis made sure he had the best of everything. Then, meeting a genuine but poor knight who was miserably caparisoned, he gave it all away.

He returned to Assisi, humiliated in the eyes of his friends but strangely buoyed up in himself. 'You'll see that one day I'll be a great prince,' was his reply to the mockery. A vision of a sumptuous hall hung with rich, knightly accoutrements had assured him that one day he would achieve his dream of glory. Moreover, he saw there a beautiful bride who would one day be his; now he was in love, without yet knowing who she would be. There was now a parting of the ways with his old companions, and to mark the occasion he gave them a sumptuous feast, the best he had ever thrown. Francis, was looking to the future, whose reality was yet unknown to him.

Rebuild my Church

Francis found himself drawn more and more to prayer, seeking out lonely spots where he could pray. During these long hours he gradually began to see the face of his beautiful lady – Lady Poverty. He became even more generous with his alms, but events showed him that poverty meant more than giving alms, or even giving away his clothes. Around this time he made a pilgrimage to Rome and was moved to pity by the sight of the many beggars there. One in particular caught his attention, one so worn down that he did not even have the will to beg. Francis gave him generous alms and was preparing to move away, then turned back. He had ridden to Rome on a magnificent horse, his clothes were of good stuff, although less flamboyant than before. By giving alms he was giving out of his abundance, especially as it was, after all, his father's. Could he give of himself even more? Could he abandon his dream of being a prince among men, strip himself of his pride and vanity? Could he become the least of men – a beggar? With the impetuosity that characterised him, Francis acted at once, stripping off his good clothes and exchanging them for the beggar's rags. He became a beggar for a day.

Meeting a leper

Francis' greatest horror was disfigurement of any sort, but above all, of leprosy. One day, riding along the road, he came face to face with that greatest fear in the shape of a hideously deformed leper. His instinct was to turn his horse and gallop off, but instead he dismounted and approached the leper, giving him all the money he had on him. Then, in an even greater gesture, he swept the man up in his arms and embraced him. He then mounted his horse to continue his journey; turning back, the leper was nowhere to be seen.

There were many leper houses in the neighbourhood, and cured completely now of his aversion Francis took delight in working among those whom he called his fellow Christians.

Repair my house

Although he perhaps did not realise it at the time, Francis was undergoing a form of novitiate, moving from his old life into a new one. One day, he stopped to pray before a crucifix in a dilapidated church called San Damiano. Suddenly the Christ on the crucifix spoke to him, saying, 'Francis, go and repair my house, which, as you can see, has fallen into ruin.' Francis took the command literally. He would repair San Damiano. Of course that would mean money, and he had none of his own, but back in his father's house were goods a-plenty. He went home and rolled up as much cloth as he could and set off for Foligno where he sold it all, as well as his horse, and offered the money to the priest to repair his church.

A noble beggar

Very wisely, the priest, realising where the money had come from, refused to take it, so Francis flung it on the window ledge where it remained. His father, meanwhile, was beside himself with rage and came after his son. He was a hard and mercenary man, but perhaps deserves some sympathy. It would not be easy for any father to see his son, on whom he had pinned such hopes, going off the rails, as he saw it, throwing his father's hard-earned money around, consorting with riff-raff and beggars, mooning around the place; perhaps he was, as some of the townsfolk were hinting, going mad.

Francis hid from his father for a whole month in a ditch by a friend's house, but eventually had the courage to come out of hiding. By this time he looked so emaciated and bedraggled that the town urchins started to throw mud and stones at him and call him names. His father, horrified to find that it was his own son who was the butt of all this ridicule, dragged him back home and chained him up in a cellar.

Pietro eventually had to leave on business, and Pica took the opportunity to release her son, thus incurring her husband's wrath and curses on his return. Pietro had had enough, and took Francis before the Bishop's court to get back his money. The Bishop ordered Francis to repay the money, which he gladly did. Then, in a grandiose gesture, Francis stripped himself completely naked, saying 'Until now I called Pietro Bernadone father, but now that I wish to serve God, I return him not only his money that he wants so much, but also the clothes I had from him.' He flung the clothes on to the ground. 'And now I can go forth naked before the Lord, saying that in all truth no longer is Pietro Bernadone my father, but my Father who is in heaven.'

Now Francis became a real beggar, going through the town with a big bowl in which people would put scraps of food.

Rebuild my Church

He still had to 'rebuild my Church', and so, without money, Francis set to and begged for the stones he needed, many of which were thrown at him, together with jeers and mockery. Most commentators have said, rightly, that Francis mistook Our Lord's meaning, that He wanted His Church to be reformed, not San Damiano to be rebuilt, but perhaps the Lord knew his 'Little Man' better than we. Francis began at the very beginning, one stone, one brick at a time. There were many people at the time, from the Pope down, who were intent on reforming the Church, which was sorely in need of it. The most urgent problem was the standard of the clergy, for if the leaders fail, then the people are shepherdless. Many priests were ill educated and illiterate, sometimes lazy and prone to sexual sin. The priest in charge of San Damiano was not one of them, but his church reflected the dismal state into which the Church had fallen.

It was appropriate, then, that Francis should start with an actual church, repairing it, clearing out the rubble and making it once again a fitting place for the worship of God. He went on to rebuild other churches, among them San Pietro, then just outside the city walls, and a little chapel in the woods, the Portiuncula.

The Order is born

It was in the Portiuncula that he received further guidance as to his vocation. Francis heard the Gospel read on the Feast of Saint Matthias, 24th February 1206, in which Jesus told his disciples, 'As you go, proclaim that the kingdom of heaven is close at hand. Cure the sick, raise the dead, cleanse the lepers, cast out devils. You received without charge, give without charge. Provide yourselves with no gold or silver, not even with a few coppers for your purses, with no haversack for the journey or spare tunic or footwear or a staff, for a workman deserves his keep'. (*Mt* 10: 7-10)

Trembling with joy, Francis realised that the Lord was speaking directly to him and exclaimed, 'This is what I wish, what I am seeking, this is what I long with all my heart to do.' He went immediately to start preaching to the people with such joy, fervour and conviction that gradually the mockery began to die down and people began to listen to a message that spoke to their hearts, to their deepest need.

Brother Bernard

One Bernard of Quintavalle, a wealthy and important resident of Assisi had been silently observing Francis, seeing his patience, his joy, his kindliness that remained steady even under severe provocation, and now he began listening to his sermons. He invited Francis to dine with him, then to stay overnight with him. Both pretended to be asleep, and Bernard watched Francis as he rose and spent the whole night in prayer, saying only 'My God and my all.' In the morning, Bernard told Francis of his desire to join him, but he wanted confirmation. They went into church to hear Mass, and afterwards opened the Missal three times. This was a practice that Francis always followed when he wanted to know the Lord's will. The first text that they read was, 'If you will be perfect, go and sell what you have and give to the poor,' the second read, 'Take nothing with you on your journey' and the third, 'If anyone wishes to come after me let him deny himself and take up his cross and follow me'.

That was enough confirmation; Bernard immediately went home and sat at his door distributing all his wealth to the poor. A priest, Sylvester, came up and told Francis that he still owed him some money for stones he had bought to restore his churches. Francis thrust a handful of gold at him, saying if he wanted more he had only to ask. Shortly afterwards Fr Sylvester joined their little band.

Others began to join him – Giles, a young peasant; a crusader Morico, who had looked after the lepers and whom Francis healed of leprosy; a knight, Angelo Tancredi. From the very beginning he was joined by men from every walk of life who gave up whatever they possessed to follow him.

The life of the brothers

The joy of their life has gone down in legend. He did not want his brothers to have dismal faces. He would later write in his Rule, 'that they should show themselves glad in the Lord, cheerful and worthy of love, and agreeable.'

Francis stipulated that all should help out at the leper hospital nearby, and they strove to earn their living by working in the fields or vineyards, or as servants, perhaps, or pursuing a craft. If they did not have enough to eat they would then beg, and give away at the end of the day whatever was left over. The humiliation of begging came hard to some, so Francis himself would do it and then gently encouraged them to try it for themselves. 'Don't think it's so difficult or humiliating,' he said. Since they were offering the people the love of God in exchange for a few scraps of bread, his brothers were giving far more than they received. In the end, the brothers vied with each other for the privilege of begging.

That summer, Francis instructed them in their way of life, moulding them to his own vision, and making them models to those who would come after them.

As their numbers increased Francis began sending them out two by two to preach in the surrounding villages, attracting their audience by singing. He told them to take their cell within them so that they should never lapse from prayer. Since not many were trained in theology he gave them a simple sermon to deliver: 'Fear and honour, praise and bless, thank and adore the Almighty Lord, the Creator of all things, the Father, the Son and the Holy Spirit. Wait no longer to confess all your sins, for death comes soon. Give and it will be given you. Forgive and you will be forgiven. Happy those who die in penitence, for theirs is the kingdom of heaven. Woe to them who will not be converted, for they will go with their father the devil into eternal fire. Be on your guard, therefore; turn from evil, and persevere to the end in that which is good.'

The brothers did not always have a good reception; some were beaten, stripped of their clothing, dragged on the ground, but gradually their patience, kindness and joy overcame their persecutors. Moreover, the people saw that they were 'one of us', living the same life of poverty.

Perfect joy

To Francis, such persecution was perfect joy because it made him most like his beloved Master. He later had a dialogue with the inaptly named 'gentle' Brother Leo:

'Brother Leo, little sheep of God, take your pen and write what is perfect joy. Supposing a messenger has come to tell me that all the Doctors of Paris have entered the Order; or if the Kings of France and England became Friars Minor, write that that will not give me perfect joy.'

Neither did perfect joy, he said, lie in working miracles, healing the sick, in having exceptional knowledge of plants and animals, for example. Instead, if he arrived at the Portiuncula cold, hungry and bleeding, if he asked for shelter and the brother did not recognise him and drove him away with blows and curses, 'That, Brother Leo, if I bear it all for the love of God, not only with patience but with happiness, convinced that I did not deserve to be treated any better, then know and remember and write it down, little sheep of God, that that is perfect joy.'

Mission and Preaching

Francis was already foreseeing a multitude of people following in his footsteps, but for the moment, in 1209 or 1210, there were twelve of them, enough to formulate a rule of life and to seek approbation for it from the Pope. Jesus had started out with only twelve apostles, so Francis would, too, and they set out joyfully for Rome.

Pope Innocent III had been Pope some twelve years. He was small, handsome, witty, intelligent, a theologian and of absolute integrity. He was determined on the reform of the Church, but his initial reaction to Francis was not favourable. He had seen other men, and movements such as the Cathars, set up to reform the Church but who, by their excess had fallen into error. Fortunately, Francis' friend the Bishop of Assisi was in Rome. Although the Bishop had doubts about the strict poverty on which Francis insisted, he introduced him to two Cardinals who would prove to be of great support to him, Giovanni de San Paolo and Ugolino. Both shared the Bishop's doubts about an Order that would exist without revenues or possessions, but Cardinal Giovanni said that if they rejected Francis' emphasis on poverty then they were rejecting the demands of the Gospel and the words of Jesus himself.

It was just before Francis' third meeting with the Pope that Innocent had a dream in which he saw a poor ragged man propping up a tottering Church, and recognised Francis as the man. He had no more doubts. He gave his verbal support to the Order, ordained Francis as a deacon – Francis always refused the honour of the priesthood – and gave the others the tonsure, thus giving them the right to preach.

Treasure of poverty

The brothers returned rejoicing to Assisi, finding themselves a dwelling of sorts in a disused leper hospital by the River Torto. It was so cramped that Francis drew chalk demarcations on the beams for his friars. Celano, the biographer of the early Franciscans, said of those days that they 'lived in perfect happiness and none of them dreamt of pitying himself.' Since they were minstrels and the troubadours of God, Francis said, 'is it not the role of the Friars Minor to comfort their neighbour in bringing him spiritual happiness?'

He did not want grumbling brothers. One day he went out with Brother Masseo and arrived at a town very hungry, so they split up to beg for food. Francis was delighted that Masseo managed to receive more than he, such great treasure. But Masseo replied, 'How can you talk about great treasure when we have no cloth, knives or plates, no servants, house or table?' Francis' reply was that they did in fact have great treasure because God had supplied it all, the bread they had been given, the fine stone of the fountain on which they were sitting for a table, and the clear water the fountain provided. 'So let us pray to God to make us love the treasure of holy poverty with all our hearts, for she is so noble that God Himself has served her.'

Creation renewed

Francis was described not as a man of prayer, but a man become prayer. There is a rabbinical saying that 'prayer restores the eighth day of creation', and in Francis this seemed to be sublimely true. In Francis there was an innocence of creation before the Fall, a simplicity and innocence that also imbued this early band of brothers. Francis' love of creation has been widely acknowledged and praised, but it was far from sentimentality, pantheism or love of creation for its own sake. Francis had achieved that rare detachment of 'having nothing, yet possessing all things' and so he made of nothing in this world a god, because all was God's. It seemed that in his own person he had already reunited a creation, damaged by the Fall, to its pristine union with God and with men. Wild creatures came tamely to him; one day birds sang so loudly that they were drowning out a sermon he was giving. Francis courteously asked them to remain silent until he finished, which they did. Even more remarkably,

Francis, seeing a flock of birds in a wood, decided he would preach to them. They came down to listen to him as he said:

My little sisters, the birds, it is your duty always and everywhere to praise God your Creator. He gives you freedom to fly everywhere and gives you double and triple raiment. He preserved your line in Noah's ark so that you would not disappear from the earth. You are even more in debt to him for the air he has given to you. You do not sow or reap, and God feeds you and gives you streams and fountains from which to drink, mountains and valleys to shelter you and lofty trees in which to nest. And since you neither spin nor sew, God clothes you and your children. Therefore your Creator loves you dearly, since he gives you so many good gifts. And so, my little sisters, do not fall into the sin of ingratitude and do not cease to give praise to God.

After he had finished, the birds once again took to the air and flew off in the form of a cross.

The wolf of Gubbio

He tamed even the most ferocious animals. In Gubbio, the townsfolk were terrorised by an enormous wolf that had taken the lives of some of them and even armed men feared to go out of the city at night. When Francis arrived in the town he had been warned about the wolf but went out with a companion to meet it, with the terrified citizens observing from the ramparts.

The wolf rushed at him, but stopped when Francis made the sign of the cross and chided him for his evil ways. The onlookers were amazed to see the wolf crouched meekly at the little man's feet while Francis and the wolf came to an agreement. The wolf would cease his attacks against the citizens of Gubbio, while Francis would ask the citizens to give the wolf whatever food he needed. This was accepted, and the wolf became a beloved addition to the town until its death.

Brother Sun and Sister Moon

Because all was God's creation, a creature of God as he was, then the sun was his brother, the moon and the running water his sisters, and every human being his brother and sister and friend. Francis sang of this in his famous *Canticle of the Creatures*, composed towards the end of his life:

All praise be Yours, all glory, all honour and all blessing,
Most High, all powerful, good Lord.
To You alone, Most High, do they belong,
No mortal lips are worthy
To pronounce Your Name

All praise be Yours, my Lord,
In all your creatures,

especially Sir Brother Sun
who brings the day;
you give us light through him.
How beautiful he is, how radiant in his splendour!
He is the token of You, Most High.

All praise be Yours, my Lord,
For Sister Moon and the Stars;
You have made them in the heavens,
bright and precious and fair.

All praise be Yours, my Lord,
for Brother Wind and the Air,
for every kind of weather, fair and stormy,
by which you nourish everything You have made.

All praise be Yours, my Lord,
For Sister Water;
so useful and lowly,
so precious and pure.

All praise be Yours, my Lord,
for Brother Fire
by whom you brighten the night.
How beautiful he is,
how merry, robust and strong!

All praise be Yours, my Lord,
for Sister Earth, our mother
who feeds us,
rules us and brings forth all manner of fruit
and coloured flowers and herbs.

The perfect friar

Francis never saw, as in Wordsworth's poem, 'a host of golden daffodils.' For him, each flower, bird or beast, was unique, to be appreciated for its own sake as created by God.

Even more so was every human being. His appreciation of the individual qualities of his brothers comes out clearly in his designation of the perfect Friar Minor: 'The good Friar Minor must love poverty like Brother Bernard and prayer like Brother Rufino, who prayed even when he slept; he must lose himself in God like Brother Giles and be courteous like Brother Angelo, as patient as Brother Juniper, that perfect image of Christ crucified; he must possess the purity and innocence of Brother Leo, the distinction and good sense of Brother Masseo, and finally resemble for charity and detachment from the world Brother Lucidus, who never stayed more than a month in the same place, since we have no abiding dwelling here below.'

Brother Angelo, former knight, earned his encomium as an outstanding example of courtesy the hard way. One day, three brigands came to the friary door demanding food and money. Brother Angelo was porter and drove them away angrily, then reported his action proudly to Francis on his return. Francis, however, was not at all congratulatory, and told him that sinners would be more likely to be won over by gentleness than condemnation and harshness. Francis gave the food he had gathered to Angelo and told him to seek out the brigands, apologise and give them the food, and ask them to reform their ways. It worked so well that the brigands did give up their robbing and live by the work of their hands; they brought firewood for the brothers and eventually became Franciscans themselves.

The peacemaker

Francis was a peacemaker. He had great success in bringing warring parties to reconciliation, especially in bringing to an end the war between Assisi and Perugia after ten years of conflict, in which he had taken part as a youth.

From the very beginning he bade his brothers greet people with the salutation 'May God give you peace,' a salutation he said was revealed to him by God. The brothers had need of this peace when one day, by the River Torto, as they were gathered in prayer, a peasant turned up with an ass and demanded that they quit the hut because he wanted to stable his beast there. Rather than argue, Francis led his little band away, homeless.

Eventually, the Benedictines who owned the little chapel of the Portiuncula heard of their plight and gave it and some surrounding land to the friars. However, as Francis steadfastly refused to own property, they compromised by 'renting' it to the brothers in return for a basket of loaches once a year.

It was an ideal place, deep in the woods, much beloved by Francis. Here the brothers built huts for themselves and their life of poverty, joy and peace continued.

Lay Followers

The Order was spreading rapidly as a loose knit fraternity. Francis began to arrange the friaries with Guardians (whom he first called Mothers) to look after the brothers. He refused to call them priors or abbots, because they were to be servants of all. Some brothers lived as hermits, others were itinerants going from town to town, so there was a great deal of flexibility.

One of the noble ladies who was impressed by Francis and his brothers and gave them alms, was the beautiful Clare Offreducci, who in 1212 was about nineteen years old. As a child she had read stories of the desert fathers and often wore a hair shirt under her sumptuous clothes. Her family wanted her to secure a good marriage, but influenced more and more by Francis' example she realised that if she wanted to follow her heart she would have to take matters into her own hands and defy her family.

On Palm Sunday 1212, dressed in all her finery she went with her family to the services at the Cathedral of San Rufino, when her courage failed her. But the following night, accompanied by Pacifica, a cousin, she slipped out of the family palace by a side door through which the dead were brought out for burial, and went to Saint Mary of the Angels where Francis was waiting for them. He cut their hair and clothed them in the coarse Franciscan habit, and lodged them for the time being with some Benedictine nuns.

Their relatives swiftly came after them but were unable to change their minds, and a few days later Clare's younger sister Agnes also ran away to join them. Their relatives were even more brutal this time, physically dragging her out of the convent and carrying her bodily down the hillside. Clare meanwhile was praying desperately for her sister's safety, when Agnes suddenly became so heavy the men were unable to hold her. Her uncle, Monaldo, was so enraged he struck her savagely, but then gave up the struggle and left the girl to return to her sanctuary. Francis received Agnes into the Franciscan Order and a short while later established this first little community of Poor Ladies, as they were called at first, at his beloved San Damiano.

Clare shared Francis' burning love for Christ and for Lady Poverty, and the spiritual kinship of Francis and Clare is one of the great 'love stories' of the Christian faith. She battled hard to keep that part of the Rule that gave them the 'privilege' of living without a fixed income or endowments, and the final papal approval for that came the day before she died.

A supper of the love of God

Clare had often asked Francis to share a meal with her, and eventually he gave way to his brothers' petitioning on her behalf to give her that happiness as a reward for her life of renunciation. She came to the Portiuncula with another sister to share supper with him and his brothers. Hardly had they begun to eat when Francis started to speak of the things of God, and the whole company fell into ecstasy. The townsfolk nearby were terrified to see flames rising from the hut and fearing it was ablaze they ran into the forest to put the fire out. As they came closer to the hut they saw the company absorbed in prayer and realised the flames were the fire of the love of God engulfing them.

The Third Order

Wherever friaries of brothers and convents of the Poor Clares were set up men and women flocked to join them, so much so that it was feared the whole of Italy would become Franciscans and the civil order be undermined. Francis' good friend Cardinal Ugolino therefore suggested to Francis that he should set up a Third Order, Tertiaries, so that people could belong to the Franciscan movement without necessarily entering the religious life. They would be encouraged to live a simple, penitential life according to the Franciscan charism in the circumstances of life in which they found themselves.

In fact, many were already doing that, though without a regular framework. One such was the noble lady Jacoba Settesoli, widow of the Knight Gratiano Frangipani, with whom Francis often stayed when he was in Rome.

Francis nicknamed her Brother Jacoba and gave her a
lamb to remind her of the Lamb of God. This lamb
followed her to church, and butted her with its head to
wake her in the morning for prayer. From its wool Jacoba
wove the habit in which Francis died. He was very fond
of a sweetmeat she made for him made from sugar and
almonds, and which he asked for on his deathbed –
known ever afterwards as *frangipani*, marzipan.

Francis had written to his lay followers, encouraging
them to live the Gospel in their lives:

> And may the Spirit of the Lord rest on all who act in
> this way, may he take up his abode within them and
> dwell with them, for they are the children of the
> Heavenly Father and do his works. They are the
> spouses, the brothers and the mothers of Our Lord
> Jesus Christ. We are his spouses when, with our souls
> sanctified by the Holy Spirit, we are united to Him. We
> are His brothers when we do the will of His Father
> who is in heaven. We are his mother when we carry
> Him in our hearts by our love and the sincerity of our
> consciences and when we give birth to him by holy
> deeds. O what glory, what dignity, grandeur to have a
> Father in heaven! What dignity, what charm, what
> happiness, what peace, what sweetness, what infinite
> joy, what supreme good fortune to have a brother who
> has given his life for His sheep!

Now he drew up a Rule of Life for them – attending Mass, receiving Holy Communion, fasting, living simply and with charity to all. It proved so popular that whole towns enrolled in the Order. It turned Italy upside down and played a great part in ending the feudal system of the Middle Ages.

A social revolution

Feudalism began during the Dark Ages as a protection against barbarian invasions. Men would bind themselves under oath to a more powerful family. The lord would pledge to give protection to the weaker one, in return for which the subordinate, the serf, was obliged to take up arms in support of his lord if necessary. The lord would also be entitled to a proportion of the serf's yield from his land. The downside was that the serf was bound to his land, making the system ever more restrictive because it deprived him of freedom of movement. However, serfdom never became the equal of slavery, because he was free to marry, to inherit property and could become quite wealthy; he was often able to purchase or be given his freedom.

The important aspect of feudalism was the oath, which was taken very seriously. However, when someone became a Franciscan tertiary the oath or vow made to God took precedence over any other, thus freeing the serf from his obligations to his overlord. Also, if a lord became a tertiary then he would often offer freedom to his serfs. At the monthly meetings of the tertiaries, something provided for in their Rule, the lord sat as an equal with the serf, the artisan with the peasant, breaking down social distinctions and barriers in the brotherhood of their Franciscan life. Besides the countless men and women of humble birth among the tertiaries there were also illustrious men and women who lived the Franciscan ideal; royalty such as Saint Louis of France and Saint Elizabeth of Hungary; many popes, priests and lay people such as the Curé of Ars, Columbus, Saint Rose of Viterbo and Margaret of Cortona; the most famous in the arts such as Dante and Michaelangelo, Petrarch and Raphael, Murillo, Palaestrina and Liszt.

Lateran Council

Eager to continue his reform of the Church, Innocent III in 1215 called the 4th Lateran Council. Innocent was one of the most powerful popes of all time, who considered that the spiritual authority of the Papacy took precedence over temporal authority, giving him authority to depose kings and princes who posed a threat to the Faith. In his conflict with the Catharists he sent an army to fight against them, but learnt from that tragic mistake that the only way to oppose error was by persuasion, good teaching, and the example of a vibrant faith and holiness of life. In Francis and Saint Dominic, founder of the Order of Preachers, he had the greatest and best of weapons he could wish for.

Both Francis and Dominic attended the Council, and met there. There could not be two men more unalike in their personalities and in their mission in the Church. Dominic was a great organiser and administrator, an outstanding preacher, and combated the various heresies spreading through France, especially, by preaching and sending out missionary priests. On the other hand, Francis was adamantly opposed to his friars becoming theologians and pursuing an academic career, because he wanted them to live a life of simplicity, poverty and prayer.

Learning or Simplicity

Cardinal Ugolino asked Francis to preach before the papal court and Pope Honorius, elected Pope after Innocent III's death in 1216, but was in an agony of apprehension lest he make himself a laughing stock. But Francis spoke with such burning love, joy and peace, almost dancing under the impulse of the Holy Spirit, that his listeners were deeply moved and impressed by his simplicity and deep humility.

A student who saw him preach in Bologna, gave an eyewitness account of that experience which gives some clue as to the impact Francis had on people:

I saw Saint Francis preach in the market place in front of the courthouse, where nearly all the town were gathered. The beginning of his sermon was 'Angels, Men, Devils'. He spoke so well and skilfully that many learned men present were not a little astonished that an unlearned man could speak like that. The whole theme of his talk was to calm dissension and create peace. His habit was dirty; his appearance insignificant, his face not handsome. But God gave his words such power that many noble families who had long been at daggers-drawn were persuaded to make peace with each other. Everyone felt such devotion and reverence for him that the crowds mobbed him, trying to take pieces of his habit or to touch the hem of his garment.

The conflict between a vocation that included learning and study and the simplicity of prayer and poverty became one of the most divisive issues for the new Order. Many of those joining had been canons, clerics and theologians and wanted to pursue their studies as before. Francis did not despise learning, provided that it did not take precedence over prayer; indeed, if he saw a piece of paper that had writing on it he would pick it up carefully and put it out of harm's way. When someone pointed out that it might contain writings of a pagan, he replied that even so, the letters would spell the name of his creator, and even pagan writings contained some truths of God.

Eventually Francis was forced to agree to some accommodation, and his attitude could be summed up in a letter he wrote to Saint Anthony of Padua who had previously been a Canon Regular and who had recently joined the Order:

> To my well-beloved Brother Anthony, Brother Francis greets you in the Lord. It pleases me that you are instructing the Brothers in holy theology, provided that this study does not quench the spirit of prayer and devotion, as it is written in the Rule. Farewell.

Saint Anthony, one of the best beloved saints of all time and a Doctor of the Church, famed for his preaching, combined holiness and learning, just as Francis would have wished. He would be followed by others, such as

Saint Bonaventure, Roger Bacon, Ockham, and Blessed Dun Scotus. The imperative was, as Francis desired, that study did not 'quench the spirit of prayer and devotion', but would foster and nourish it. As he told his friars, 'Go out and spread the Gospel, and if necessary, preach.'

Trusting in God

On the other hand, Dominic learnt from Francis. He attended the Franciscan Chapter, one called the 'Chapter of the Mats' because there were so many friars attending, some five thousand, that many had to sleep out under the stars on roughly woven mats. After addressing the brothers, Francis exhorted them to give themselves to prayer and worship of God without thinking of bodily nourishment, 'since Christ has expressly undertaken to provide it.'

Dominic was horrified at such imprudence, failing to provide food for such a large number of hungry men, but then he saw people converging from all the villages around with donkeys and mules laden with food for the friars. They even provided plates and drinking cups. Dominic resolved that his friars, too, should follow evangelical poverty. The greatest theologians could also be deeply humble as the Dominicans would also prove. Saint Thomas Aquinas, after writing most of his *Summa Theologia*, had a vision of Christ. He wrote no more, saying that all he had written was as straw.

Respect for the Church

At the Lateran Council, Francis would have mingled with the greatest prelates of the Church, no novelty for him, as he often went to Rome. He could not have been unaware of the worldliness of a good many of the bishops, cardinals and other clerics of the papal court, of whom it was said that no word of religion passed their lips. The money-grabbing of many of them, their search for worldly power and esteem, even their immorality, often caused scandal, but he never spoke a word of criticism. Early in his conversion, Francis had received supernatural assurance that his sins were forgiven, but he never saw himself as other than a sinner with the rest of humankind; therefore he would never pass judgment, only preach repentance. It was the example of his own radiant holiness that attracted people and made them want to turn their backs on their old life and seek holiness in their turn.

Holiness of Francis

Francis once chanted a very special Office with Brother Leo. He told Leo to chant:

'Brother Francis, you have committed so many sins during your life in the world that you undoubtedly deserve hell.'

Brother Leo sang:

'And you now do so much good that you will certainly go to heaven.'

Francis told him he had to repeat what he had said, not make up words of his own, and continued;

'Brother Francis, the sins you are guilty of against the Lord of Heaven and Earth are so great that you deserve to be damned through all eternity.'

Brother Leo sang:

'And you will make, thanks to God, such progress in virtue that you will deserve to be blessed through all eternity.'

Annoyed, Francis told him that by holy obedience he must repeat his words exactly, and continued:

'Miserable Francis, tremble for not having found grace in the Lord's sight, for you have so gravely offended the God of all good and the Father of all consolation – and you must respond that it is perfectly true that I am unworthy of pardon.'

'Very well, replied Brother Leo, 'I will then respond that God whose goodness is still greater than our sins will assuredly pardon you.'

Francis then asked him why he did not respond as he was told, and Brother Leo replied, 'My father, God is my witness that I try to repeat your words, but Our Lord Himself puts other words into my mouth.'

On another occasion, when Francis arrived in a town and was led in as in a triumphal procession, with people greeting him as a saint, Brother Masseo kept asking him why people persisted in coming after him, why everyone wanted to see him and hear him. How did Francis keep his humility?

Francis replied that God had not seen anyone who was a greater sinner than he was and chose him to confound the nobleness, the greatness, the strength and the beauty and wisdom of the world, so that everyone would know that all virtue and goodness came from Him and not from the creature; that no-one could glory in himself, but in the Lord.

Love for the Eucharist

He saw clearly that while he was, in his eyes, vile and unworthy, God had overwhelmed him with his graces, and he was also aware that in the Church there were unworthy ministers. Yet he recognised that the inestimable treasure Christ had entrusted to his Church still ran pure and clear from its fount for all those who would receive what Christ willed to give them, despite the unworthiness of the ministers charged with dispensing it. The greatest treasure was the Holy Eucharist. Francis received the Sacred Host with such reverence that many were drawn to a deeper love and reverence for it, too. This is why he loved and respected even the humblest of priests, because, he explained, 'I see nothing corporally of the Most High Son of God save his most Holy Body and Blood which they receive and which they alone have the power to administer.'

One day a Manichean brought to his attention the conduct of a priest who was living with a woman and asked him whether he had to believe in this priest's teaching and respect the sacraments he administered. Francis went to the priest and knelt before him. 'I do not know whether these hands are stained, as the other man claims,' he said. 'In any case, I do know that even if they are, this in no way lessens the power and efficacy of the sacraments of God. That is why I kiss them out of respect for what they administer and out of respect for Him who delegated his authority to them.'

Pope Innocent dies

Pope Innocent III died 16th July 1216, the year after calling the Lateran Council. He had bestrode the world, but he had hardly drawn his last breath before his courtiers deserted him, robbers broke into the church at Perugia where his body lay and stole everything from it, leaving it abandoned on the ground. It was left to Francis to travel to Perugia, to pray and weep as a son, with pity and gratitude, for one who had truly been, not just the Pope, but a wise and loving father in Christ to him.

The Pope had instigated measures to reform the Church with the power and authority given to him; his spiritual son Francis was the example given by God to show men and women how the Christ-life could be lived. The Church needed both Pope and 'Poverello' if it were to fulfil better its mission to show the face of Christ to the world. Pope and 'Poverello' worked together for this reform, with the wisdom of the Church providing the guidance and structure that the genius of Francis needed for his ideal to remain true.

Crusading Knight

Following the Council, Francis was eager for his Order to spread beyond Italy, and this resolution was passed at the Pentecost Chapter of 1217. His first choice was, understandably, France, because, he said, it was the country that most reverenced the Holy Eucharist, and, of course, he was enamoured of its troubadour tradition. He was on his way when Cardinal Ugolino met with him to dissuade him. There were some prelates, he explained to Francis, who were much opposed to him, and he could not guarantee his protection further afield. Reluctantly Francis submitted, sending Brother Pacificus, who had been a troubadour, in his place. Cardinal Ugolino had good grounds for concern, because initially, friars going into Germany and Hungary were very badly treated, some were killed, and many had to return to Italy. They had much better success in England, where they soon became established and respected. The Order just did not have at that time the necessary structures in place to give them credence.

Following the Crusade

During the Council, the Pope had called for a new Crusade to the Holy Land to regain the Holy Places, especially the Tomb of Christ, and Francis decided to embark with the army. He had tried a few times before to go to the east, but each time had had to turn back due either to bad weather or sickness. It was now Honorius III, Innocent III's successor, who launched the 5th Crusade in 1217. Innocent had made the Tau, the 'T' shaped cross, the sign of the Crusade, and ever after Francis, too, adopted it as his sign.

On 24th June 1219, Francis and twelve friars set sail for Damietta, a town in Egypt, which the Crusaders had been besieging for a year. If they could take the town, then they could go on to Cairo which would cause the whole of Egypt to fall. The Crusaders were eager to make a final assault, but Francis spent the whole night in prayer before the battle, and he discerned that they would be defeated. He asked one of his companions if he should make his prophecy known to the commanders. 'If I tell them, they will think me a fool, but if I say nothing my conscience will trouble me,' he said. 'You've been thought a fool many times,' his companion replied, so obey your conscience and God, not men.'

Francis did so and the commanders respected his advice, but the soldiers laughed at him, eager for battle and the spoils they would win. Francis was proved right and the Muslims gained a victory of sorts, although seriously weakened. While in the Crusader camp Francis had his usual success in drawing men to conversion, with some even joining the Franciscans.

Meeting the Sultan

After the battle Francis took advantage of a truce to obtain reluctant permission from the Papal Legate to cross the lines and speak with Sultan al-Malik al-Kamil, ruler of Egypt, Syria and Palestine. His intention was simple – to convert the Sultan and save his soul, and so he could win back the Holy Land for the Christians. It was a courageous thing to do, because the Sultan had ordered that a gold piece should be given for the head of every Christian slain.

Undeterred, he set off boldly, and eager also for martyrdom, with Brother Illuminato as interpreter. He bolstered his companion's courage by pointing out two lambs grazing in a field that he took for a sign of God's protection. When they reached the Saracen lines the guards seized them and beat them severely, with the two friars shouting 'Soldan, Soldan'. They were dragged in chains before the Sultan, just as they wished.

The cruel beast became sweetness itself, the wolf became transformed into a lamb, faced with the person of Saint Francis, said the commentators of this meeting. The Sultan was intrigued by this ragged little man, so on fire and joyous with the love of God, who declared he had come to proclaim the Gospel of Jesus Christ and to save the Sultan's soul by converting him. In response, the Sultan summoned his imams and offered to debate with

Francis, but he declined this offer. 'Our faith is greater than human reason,' he replied. 'Reason is of no use unless a person believes.'

Tests and trials

Francis and Illuminato stayed perhaps a month or so in the Saracen camp. Illuminato testified that the Sultan said that he believed 'that your faith is good and true', but pointed out the difficulties of his conversion. His own life would be at risk as well as that of the two friars, so it would be impossible to convert. Francis then challenged him. Let an imam and Francis himself pass through fire to prove whose faith deserved to be held as the holier and the more certain. The Sultan saw his imams quietly melting away, beginning with the eldest, and told Francis frankly that he did not think any of them would be willing to undergo such a test. He also declined a further offer that Francis put: that only he pass through the fire; if he died, then attribute it to his sins, if he survived, then let the Sultan acknowledge that Christ is the power and wisdom of God as true God and Saviour of all.

Instead, the Sultan set up some tests of his own. He had a carpet laid in front of him, decorated with a pattern of crosses. Francis would have to tread over the cross-patterned carpet to speak with the Sultan, and thus show contempt for his crucified Lord, or decline to do so and thus insult the Sultan. Francis entered and strode boldly across the carpet and the Sultan pointed out to him his desecration of the Cross of Christ.

'Not so,' replied Francis. 'Thieves also were crucified with Christ. We Christians have the true Cross, which we venerate with great devotion, so what you have are the crosses of the thieves. That is why I do not hesitate to walk over the symbols of brigands.'

The Sultan then quoted the scriptures and asked why the Crusaders did not turn the other cheek, and pay back evil for good, as Jesus demanded – not realising that he, presumably unwittingly, was putting the Islamic invasion of Christian lands in the 'evil' camp. The Sultan had obviously not read all of the Gospel passage, (*Mt* 5), Francis replied, because it went on to say that if your eye offended you, pluck it out, and if your hand offended you, cut it off. So, if Muslims tried to draw Christians away from their faith, then they should be expelled.

The Sultan finally offered Francis money and rich gifts, which Francis refused, even when the Sultan said he could give them to poor Christians. All he would accept was an ivory horn, and a pass that would allow the two of them to go through Saracen-occupied lands without harm and would also exempt them from the tax that Islamic law levied on non-Muslims. But he left with the Sultan's admiration and respect, who looked upon him as a man different from all others. As a mark of the Sultan's respect, Franciscans since then became guardians of the Holy Places.

Return to the Crusader camp

The Sultan provided an armed escort and an honour guard for their return to the Christian lines, a measure of his esteem. With his pass, Francis was able to travel throughout the east to the Holy Land, visiting Christian shrines and the places connected with the life of Christ. The records do not speak of this, and perhaps wisely so. Who could put into words what this meant for Francis, being in the same places sanctified by his beloved Lord?

Was Francis' attempt to convert the Sultan fruitless? It seems not. The *Fioretti* recount that before returning to Italy Francis met with the Sultan again, who confided that he did want to become a Christian, but that he was already meeting with opposition from his people for being too tolerant towards Christians, and not a fervent enough Muslim. Francis then told him that after his – Francis' – death, two friars would be inspired to travel to him, to instruct him and baptise him. This took place about twelve years after Francis' death and when the Sultan was on own death-bed.

Storm Clouds

Francis and his party were resting at St Jean d'Acre on their way home when a friar, Brother Stefano the Simple, caught up with them as the bearer of bad news. During Francis' prolonged absence and with some thinking he had died, the Order was in crisis. The problems had been there ever since the Order had expanded beyond the dedicated handful of his earliest followers. Many Franciscans had never met Francis, had not imbibed his spirit, and now wanted to go their own ways. Besides those who wanted to continue with a life of learning – which was badly needed to properly train those entering the priesthood – there were also those who were unable or unwilling to follow Francis' path of absolute poverty. Others wanted more structure and organisation in the Order. All these differing forces had now gained the upper hand.

A new authority

A Chapter had been called in which these measures were put into practice. The Provincial, Peter of Stacia, established an imposing House of Studies in Bologna that rivalled that of the Dominicans. Stringent Constitutions were drawn up, multiplying the times of fasting and abstinence and tightening up procedures and discipline. To some extent these measures were needed, because anyone could join, there was no novitiate, and some friars could and did cause scandal by living as vagabonds. Francis called them 'Brother Fly'.

Any friar who protested against these measures, so contrary to what Francis had envisaged, was thrown out of the Order or had to go into hiding to escape the wrath of those now in authority. Among these were Francis' closest companions, including his first companion, Brother Bernard, and also Brother Stefano, who carried with him a copy of the new Constitutions. Francis read them as he sat at table with Peter Catanii ready to eat. A dish of meat had been prepared for them, but according to the Constitution it was a day of abstinence. 'Peter, what shall we do then?' Francis asked. 'We will do what you wish, for you are the one who can command,' he replied. 'Then let us eat the meat, in the freedom of the Holy Gospel.'

Lady Poverty in peril

Francis left St Jean d'Acre straight away, stopping at Bologna where he was so incensed at the new building that he started to tear down the roof with his bare hands. The podesta was summoned and pointed out that the property was not his but the community's. He then went straight on to Rome, his arrival in Italy greeted with joy and relief by his faithful friars, to speak with the Pope about the problems of the Order. At Francis' request, the Pope gave him Cardinal Ugolino as Protector, who would help restore equilibrium to the troubled Order.

Ugolino was always a faithful friend to Francis and was wise enough to know that with the Order now so widespread it was vital that a new Rule be drawn up that would be more structured than Francis' original Rule, but more flexible than the one drawn up in his absence. This Rule of 1221 was more a manual of spiritual instruction and was rejected by the Holy See. Francis therefore retired to Fonte Colombo with his faithful 'little lamb of God', Brother Leo, to fast and pray and re-write the Rule. He was by now a very sick man. An eye condition had been exacerbated by his stay in the hot, dry lands of the east, even though the Sultan had given him remedies.

Rule of 1223

If Francis thought he would have some peace in his retreat he was to be disappointed. Friars from both sides of the argument came to him, pleading or insisting on their cause. Brother Elias was chosen as the spokesman for those who had heard that Francis was writing a new Rule and, knowing how austere he was towards himself, was afraid that he would impose a harsh regime on them.

Those closest to the Poverello wanted to keep his original vision of absolute poverty and simplicity of life; others insisted that very few could sustain such a life, with some justification. The 'convents' at this time, for example, were at best rough wooden or wattle huts or caves, a way of life too extreme for most. Francis worked with Cardinal Ugolino to produce the Rule of 1223, which the Holy See accepted as definitive. It had enough flexibility to allow those who wished to live in absolute poverty to do so, while allowing others to have suitable houses and permission to study.

Nevertheless it nearly broke Francis. So enamoured was he of his Lady Poverty that it tore him apart to see her fair face despoiled, and occasioned the few incidences of harshness in him. When a friar came to him with a coin given as alms, for example, Francis made the Brother put it on a piece of dung with his mouth.

While remaining the ultimate authority in the eyes of all, in 1220 Francis had relinquished his place as Minister General of the Order to Peter Catanii, who sadly died shortly afterwards, and his place was taken by Brother Elias. He was the leader of those who wanted the Order to own property, to study, to become more like the other religious orders. It was he who oversaw the Basilica of Saint Francis in Assisi. His ambition almost destroyed the Order after Francis' death.

It was difficult for Francis to see many of his beloved brothers slipping further away from his original ideals until the Lord spoke reassuringly to him: 'Poor Little Man,' the Voice said, 'why are you sad? Is not your Order my Order?

Am I not its chief shepherd? Stop troubling yourself and look rather to your own salvation.' Francis was assured, then, that his Order was in more than good hands.

Francis' great temptation

This period of his life was the hardest he had endured and Francis, ill and at the end of his endurance, slipped into a profound depression. He doubted his vocation to a life of absolute poverty. Had he been inspired by God in insisting on it, or deluded? Worse, was he being disobedient by insisting on it against the advice of Cardinal Ugolino, who represented the authority of the Church, which had always been his guiding star in showing him the will of God? To add to his agony of spirit, the presence of God, which had been so luminous to him, had gone. He was in profound darkness, with no sense of God's presence. Was that because of his sins and disobedience? He multiplied his prayers, his fasting, his penances, treating with harshness the one creature, his body, 'Brother Ass', for which he had never had compassion, although he forbade his friars to indulge in excessive penance themselves.

This two year period of trial ended when the Lord once again spoke to him, 'Francis, if you had faith like a grain of mustard seed, you would say to this mountain "go", and it would obey you.' 'What is this mountain, Lord?' 'It is the mountain of temptation.' 'Lord,' Francis replied, 'let it be done according to Your Word.' The temptation melted away like snow and his former peace, serenity and joy returned to him.

The crib of Greccio

His spirits once more restored, Francis saw the Rule given Papal approbation on 29th November 1223. Free of responsibilities, his thoughts turned to Christmas which he called 'the feast of feasts'. It combined his love of poverty, and the smallness of God become flesh in a tiny baby held in the arms of the Virgin Mary, for whom he had the tenderest love. Giovanni Velita, the Lord of Greccio, had become a Franciscan, and possessed a mountain opposite the town, which was punctuated by caves and a small wood. It made an ideal setting where Francis could reproduce the stable at Bethlehem 'in such a way as to represent as perfectly as possible the suffering and hardship He endured as a baby to save us. That is why I want you to set up on this spot a real crib with some hay, with an ox and an ass.'

On Christmas Eve, from their vantage point high on the mountain, friars gathered round the crib saw ribbons of light as the people climbed up the mountain from all around to the Crib where Mass was celebrated and Francis assisted, as deacon; he preached the sermon, his voice strong and clear, filled with joy and delight. Giovanni Vella testified that at one point the figure of Jesus in the crib opened its eyes and gazed upon Francis and smiled at him.

Wounds of Christ

Francis spent a few more weeks at Greccio, attended the Chapter in June, then later that summer made his way to a mountain called La Verna, taking with him some of his most trusted and closest companions.

Ten years earlier, Francis had been at a tourney. The sight must have stirred his blood, seeing the jousting knights, the richly dressed lords and ladies, the pennants fluttering gaily in the breeze, the caparisoned horses pawing at the ground. Francis and his companion, clothed in their gray-brown habits, stood on a low wall and sang 'So great is the happiness I look for, that every pain is a pleasure'. Their joy impressed everyone, especially one of those present, the lord Orlando of Chiusi. He approached Francis and offered him a mountain he owned, which the brothers could use to make hermitages – Mount La Verna. Now ten years on, Francis climbed this mountain where he would experience his beloved Lord in a unique way.

The group journeyed to the mountain in the stifling August heat; Francis was so weak and ill that he rode on a donkey. Once there, they were welcomed by Count Orlando and built themselves hermitages among the stunning scenery that Francis could now hardly see.

Weakened as he was, Francis decided to keep a forty day fast from the Feast of the Assumption (15th August) to the Feast of St Michael, (29th September) and withdrew into even greater solitude. Only Brother Leo was permitted to come to him daily with his meagre food.

It was a period of ecstasy and agony, the most intense union of love with Love Himself, and grievous torments from the devil, a period of deepest purification that would prepare him for what was to come. There were touches of respite – a falcon that came and nested next to his cell and an angel who came to play him the most exquisite music, the loveliness of which was so great that 'I thought I should have fainted if the angel had drawn his bow once more, and my soul would have left my body,' Francis testified, 'so far did my happiness exceed human limits that I could bear.'

Stigmata

On the Feast of the Exaltation of the Holy Cross, 14th September, just before dawn, Francis knelt in prayer. 'Lord, I ask two graces of you before I die: to experience myself, as far as possible, the sufferings of your cruel Passion, and to have the selfsame love for you that caused you to sacrifice yourself for me.'

Suddenly, a seraph swept down from heaven towards him. In its midst was the figure of a man hanging on a cross. Two of the seraph's wings were at the head, two served for flight, two covered the body. The Prophet Isaiah (chapter 6) had a similar vision of God on his throne in the midst of a six-winged seraph. Saint John the Evangelist said this was a vision of Christ (*Jn* 12:41). Now, Francis saw him as the crucified Christ. When the vision ended, Francis saw that his body bore the wounds of the crucifixion in his hands, feet and side, the blood seeping through his tunic.

Covering the wounds, Francis sought out his brothers and asked them whether extraordinary graces should be revealed. 'Brother Francis,' said Brother Illuminato, 'it may be wrong for you to keep to yourself what God has intended for the edification of all.' Francis then revealed what had happened to him, but Brother Leo, who nursed him and washed his wounds, was the only one permitted to see them while he was alive.

The following day, in the midst of the pain of his wounds, Francis sang of his joy in praise of his Creator:

All holy are You, Lord God, God of gods;
Sole Maker of all miracles; strong and great!
Highest are You, and All-Powerful;
You are the Father, King of Heaven and earth,
Trinity and Unity, Lord, God of gods.

You are the perfect Good, sole, highest Good;
True and only Lord, living God.
You are Love, Wisdom, Patience, Joy,

Security, Beauty, Justice Quietude.
You are Humility, You are our Hope,
Our Temperance and our Peace, our Fortitude.

You are the only riches we need,
Our discipline, our protection and our guard,
Our refuge, our sure defence and strength.
You are our Faith and Hope and Love.

You are our spring of sweetness welling up,
You, mighty source of infinite goodness.
Omnipotent Lord God, mysterious, high,
Loving and merciful, our dear Saviour, Christ!

With Clare at Damiano

Francis was taken back to his Portiuncula. News of his stigmata spread, and many came to venerate him; miracles flowed out through his emaciated body. In the summer of 1225 Francis agreed to return to his hermitage of Rieti, but when he reached San Damiano he was so sick that he stayed there for six weeks where Clare and her sisters, nursed him devotedly. Even here, his torments were not ended. The hut in which he lay was overrun by mice and tested even Francis' love of God's creatures. Almost at the end of his tether he cried out to his Lord. 'Francis,' the Lord replied, 'if instead of all your sufferings you received a treasure besides which the whole earth, even if made of gold would be worth nothing, would you not have reason to be content?'

'Assuredly, Lord.'

'Then be happy, I promise you that one day you will enjoy the Kingdom of Heaven, and that is as certain as if you already possessed it.'

The following morning Francis sang to his brothers his 'Canticle of the Creatures'. He said they should sing it as they went on their missions, and he now frequently bade them sing it to him to take his mind off his sufferings and turn him to praise of his Creator.

Cauterisation

Francis was moved to Rieti, where healings and miracles continued. His eye problems were causing him such distress that it was decided to try an extreme treatment – to cauterise the flesh with a red hot iron above the most afflicted eye, from the ear to the eyebrow. Even Francis' heroic courage almost failed him at this point, but he remembered his love for his 'brother fire'. As they brought the glowing iron to him he addressed his brother: 'My Brother Fire, noble and useful, whom I have always loved, for the love of him who created you, be courteous to me now, temper your heat so that I can bear it.' Just as the wind and waves were obedient to their Lord Jesus, so now Brother Fire was obedient to Francis, and he felt no pain as the treatment was administered.

Sister Death

It was obvious to all that Francis' life was drawing to a close, and everyone wanted the honour of his presence, especially at his death. Francis wanted to die at the Portiuncula, the Assisans wanted to claim their venerated son for themselves. Assisi won. The whole city turned out to greet him, and his return turned into a triumphal procession.

His body was totally ravaged by sickness, but his spirit soared. He now added to the Canticle of the Creatures a further stanza to Sister Death:

Praised be my Lord for our Sister the Death of the Body,
From whom no man escapes.
Woe to him who dies in mortal sin.
Blessed are those who are found walking by Your most holy Will,
For the second death will have no power to harm them.

To the last he was a peacemaker. When a quarrel broke out between the bishop of Assisi and the mayor, Francis sent his brothers into the city square to sing his 'Canticle of the Creatures', to which he added a further strophe:

All praise be yours, my Lord,
For those who forgive one another for love of you,
And endure infirmity and tribulation.

Happy they who endure these things in peace,
For they will be crowned by you, Most High.

And he brought about their reconciliation.

Some of the townsfolk were scandalised at the singing emanating from Francis' room, thinking he should be meditating on his last end with greater seriousness, but Francis was unrepentant. He had moved through the world singing the praises of his God, and he would die singing. This was despite his atrocious suffering; he confessed that the cruellest martyrdom would be less tolerable than just three days of what he was suffering, yet he was at peace, preferring God's permissive will above all.

As his days drew to their end, Francis asked to be taken to the Portiuncula, the beloved little church of Saint Mary of the Angels. As he was carried up he asked for his litter to be turned so that he could face the city of his birth that lay nestled below him, although he could no longer see it. He blessed it, that 'she may be for ever the place and dwelling of those who acknowledge you truly and glorify your blessed and most glorious name, for ever and ever. Amen.'

Arriving at the Portiuncula he also blessed that place, which he said should forever hold a special place in the affection and veneration of his followers.

Naked I came, naked I shall return

His thoughts were all with those whom he loved – in other words, everyone and every creature, and especially those closest to him. He asked that his first follower, Bernard Quintavalle, should be loved and revered with special affection; that Sister Clare should not mourn his death 'for I promise her that she and her sisters shall see me again.' He also wanted to see 'Brother Jacoba' again, and for her to bring him a shroud of haircloth for his burial; she forestalled him and arrived before the messenger had set off, bringing with her exactly what he wanted. This included his favourite sweetmeat of marzipan, but he was only able to taste it and Bernard finished it for him.

As evening drew near on Saturday, 3rd October he asked to be laid out naked on the ground, in the utmost poverty, but also perhaps in the original innocence of our first parents. He then started to intone Psalm 142, 'With all my voice I cried to the Lord,' which those gathered round him continued. 'Bring my soul out of this prison that I may give thanks to your name.' As his soul passed to the God who created him, a flock of crested larks rose up into the air. Francis had always loved those little sisters of his with a special affection because their dun coloured feathers and crested heads reminded him of the Franciscan habit; now they were privileged to mourn his passing.

His body was brought back into Assisi the following day, and as the cortège passed San Damiano Sister Clare and her sisters came out to reverence his body. That body seemed already to share in the glory that was now his in heaven; it had previously been shrunken and browned by his suffering, but now his limbs became as supple as those of a child; his face, so scarred by the burning and wizened by pain, became angelically beautiful, his whole body became milky white, with the wounds of the stigmata shining like black pebbles.

Two years later the Church confirmed what all already knew, and Francis' old friend Cardinal Ugolino, elected Pope as Gregory IX the previous year, raised him to the altars as Saint Francis of Assisi.

Canticle of the Creatures

All praise be yours, Most High, all powerful, good Lord.
All glory, all honour and all blessing,
To you alone, Most High, do they belong,
No mortal lips are worthy
To pronounce your Name.

All praise be yours, my Lord,
In all your creatures,
Especially Sir Brother Sun
Who brings the day;
You give us light through him.
How beautiful he is, how radiant in his splendour!
He is the token of you, Most High.

All praise be yours, my Lord,
For Sister Moon and the Stars;
You have made them in the heavens,
Bright and precious and fair.

All praise be yours, my Lord,
For Brother Wind and the Air,
For every kind of weather, fair and stormy,
By which you nourish everything you have made.

All praise be yours, my Lord,
For Sister Water;

So useful and lowly,
So precious and pure.

All praise be yours, my Lord,
For Brother Fire
By whom you brighten the night.
How beautiful he is,
How merry, robust and strong!

All praise be yours, my Lord,
For Sister Earth, our mother
Who feeds us, rules us and brings forth all manner of fruit
And coloured flowers and herbs.

All praise be yours, my Lord,
For those who forgive one another for love of you
And endure infirmity and tribulation.
Happy they who endure these things in peace
For they will be crowned by you, Most High.

All praise be you, my Lord,
For our Sister the Death of the Body,
From whom no man escapes.
Woe to him who dies in mortal sin.
Blessed are those who are found walking by Your most
holy Will,
For the second death will have no power to harm them.